How to Survive
Probation

How to Survive Probation

SECRETS TO SUCCESS FOR CRIMINAL STATE AND COUNTY PROBATION

Tim Clay

To order additional copies of this book, contact:
Xlibris Corporation
1-888-795-4274
www.Xlibris.com
Orders@Xlibris.com
89881

CONTENTS

INTRODUCTION

On August 15, 2001, two brothers waited by the phone. It rang.

"How much do you need? We don't have that much. Okay, that will work, what time can you be here? No, I don't want to come to you, you come to me. Okay, fine then, but not at your place. We'll call you when we get close with instructions."

The two brothers drove to the growing town just southeast of Nashville and went to a local restaurant.

"I don't like this, maybe we should call the whole thing off," one said.

"Maybe, but I can't imagine he'd set us up. We've known each other for years."

"Well, let's do this." And the call was made.

Fifteen minutes later, Josh L. arrived. Something was off in his clothing, but neither brother could place what it could be. He was shaking, but he always shook.

"Stick to the plan" were the last words that could be spoken before Josh reached their table.

The plan was simple. One brother would go to the bathroom with Josh and get the money. The second brother would then leave with Josh and require him to enter public establishments before the drugs would be given, thus disrupting the line of sight of any surveillance.

Did the plan work? No. Perhaps if this or that were changed it would have worked, but having almost $10K in police money in your pocket is a little hard to explain. The brothers were arrested for sale of a schedule I narcotic, ecstasy, and later received a sentence of eight years, eight months in jail, the balance on probation with 1600 hours of community service work and random drug testing. Additionally, one brother was ordered to continue drug counseling.

So why tell this story? Because both brothers are not only successful in their probation but in their personal lives as well.

*   *   *

The year 2000 was quite interesting for me. We survived the infamous Y2K bug that was destined to wipe out life as we knew it. I went to my first and only Mardi Gras. I met the woman who would later become my wife. And I became a probation officer.

Like everything I did in life I wanted to be the best. I learned all I could about warrants, sentencing, community service, rules of probation, the different judges' tendencies, and the science of drug testing.

During the ten months I was a probation officer, I always won my cases. I was always prepared, had my evidence in order, and always knew I was right when I decided to file a warrant.

A probation officer has incredible discretion as to what constitutes a violation of probation. If a person misses the scheduled reporting time due to illness, but they called first, is a doctor's note necessary? How many late payments should be allowed before issuing a warrant? And the list goes on and on.

What kind of probation officer was I? I was very strict. Everything was black and white. You either obeyed the rules or I filed a warrant. Missed appointments required a doctor's note, and I would call the doctor to make sure it wasn't a forgery. Passed a drug test? I'd give another a week later just to see if they partied to celebrate beating the drug screen. Like many probation officers, I believed my job was to vigorously search for violations, while facilitating the court-ordered conditions of the probation. This is called as the "punishment" philosophy. That was my personality.

There are *many* different personalities in the probation offices around the country. Some are very laid back. Some are very rigid. Most are somewhere in between. I worked in a small town where things are much different than the big city. Some POs think it's *their* job to punish you for your crime, whereas most recognize their job is to supervise your becoming a productive citizen again. The important thing to remember is that a PO is a person who has their own personality, their own personal biases, and their own idea of what their job is.

You cannot change the way your probation officer is, thinks, or behaves, so don't try. All you can do is make sure you do what YOU need to do to stay out of jail. The bottom line is this—YOUR PROBATION OFFICER CANNOT FILE A WARRANT UNLESS YOU GIVE THEM A REASON!

According to the US Justice Statistics, nationally, only 57 percent of those on probation successfully complete their sentence. That's freaking insane! Forty-three percent of all probationers end up violating their probation? And 18 percent of people on probation end up incarcerated either for violating the terms of probation or for a new offense.

This is nuts!

I say this with confidence, conviction, and passion—YOU CAN MAKE IT THROUGH PROBATION! If you do all the things described in this book, you WILL make it.

I have the unique perspective of not only being a probation officer but also of being on probation. *I* was one of the brothers described earlier. In the past six years I completed 1600 hours of community service work, was the general manager of a multimillion-dollar corporation, experienced the joy of having children (and the headaches), and faced many challenges financially, spiritually, in my marriage, and with various temptations. I am by no means perfect—far from it. But I recognize my limitations and strive to make the right choices.

This book is written for one purpose: to help you or someone you love survive probation. Not just to stay out of jail, but make it through with no warrants and no violation reports. And ultimately, to help you be successful in relationships, work, and life.

Are you ready? Read on.

CHAPTER 1

USEFUL TIPS

For many reading this book this is your first time in trouble with the law. Up to this point you have either stayed out of trouble or been slick enough not to get caught. For others, this is part of an ongoing cycle. Either way, I wanted to start off with some basic tips for those at the beginning of the probation process. If you have been on probation a while, you will still benefit from some of these tips.

Your First Appointment

As in every other relationship in life, first impressions are everything. With probation you get two chances to make that first impression. The first is when you meet your probation officer in court. The second is your first official meeting.

This first contact usually involves a brief interview where your probation officer takes some basic information. It is usually brief, and your probation officer will give you instructions about your first reporting date.

It is *very* important to pay attention to these instructions. You may be distracted with everything going on, but it is critical that you go to the first appointment with any requested documentation, NO MATTER WHAT! Also, be sure to ask and verify what you need to bring with you. Write it down or ask them to write it down for you. And be sure to keep all the paperwork they give you in court.

If you avoided jail or prison time during sentencing, then your first report will likely be within the first two weeks of your court date. You need to be well-groomed and prepared with any documentation required.

If you were sentenced to jail or prison, you will likely be required to notify your probation officer within twenty-four to seventy-two hours of release. This can sometimes be tricky as you will see in the following true story.

Joe was released from the county jail after serving five months in jail. He had seven years of probation and was told to call his probation officer within twenty-four hours of release. He did.

He called his probation officer the morning he was released and got her voicemail. He left a message that he was released and needed to make an appointment to report. No reply. The next afternoon he called again, no reply. He then sent a letter, certified mail, to his probation officer stating that he had been released and needed to report. He sent copies of the letter to both the judge in the case and to the supervisor of the state probation office. Finally, his probation officer called and set the appointment.

What would have happened if Joe was not relentless in his attempts to contact his probation officer? What if he hadn't sent the certified letter? We may not know the answer to the question, but we do know one thing for sure. Had his probation officer filed a warrant for failure to report, Joe would have provided documentation that *she* was a liar!

The other thing we know for sure, had she filed a warrant, and he didn't have documentation backing his word that he attempted to contact her, *he* would have been spending the next seven years in prison.

Let me make this clear. If it is your word against the probation officer's word, you will lose the case. You *have* to have documentation for everything you do—more on this in a bit.

I suggest the following steps for those who are being released from prison or jail and need to schedule an appointment.

1. **Call your probation officer as soon as you are released** or as soon as the probation office opens.
2. **Use a cell phone or other phone where you have access to the phone records if needed in court.** Even without sending the certified letter, Joe's probation officer would have had a difficult time winning a court case when phone records showed he called multiple times.
3. **Call every day until you reach the probation officer.** If that doesn't work, then after 3 days . . .

4. **Ask to speak to your probation officer's supervisor.** If you speak to the supervisor, be polite and state your name, the reason for your call (need to report ASAP and PO will not return your calls), and desired result (an appointment). If you are unable to reach the supervisor, then . . .

5. **Send a letter via US Postal service** to your probation officer requesting an appointment. Send copies of the letter to the judge and the State Probation office. If you are on some sort of private probation, send it to the main office of the private probation company. **ALL LETTERS SHOULD BE SENT CERTIFIED MAIL with RETURN RECEIPT REQUESTED!**

6. **Avoid ANY alcohol or drugs before your first appointment.**

I'll talk more about avoiding drugs later, but it is critical that you not only avoid drugs, but alcohol as well. It is VERY tempting to go out and celebrate your jail release. You may think, *What's a few drinks going to hurt?*

It's going to hurt a lot if it lands you back in jail. For the average man, if you drink six beers between 12:00 a.m. and 3:00 a.m., you will still be legally drunk at 7:00 a.m., the time most probation offices open. If you get a call saying to report by nine or ten, depending on your weight, and more importantly your metabolism, you may very well still be legally drunk. Even if you are not, it does not set a good first impression to report to your first meeting smelling like alcohol.

I go into much greater detail in the chapter on reporting. It is one of the most important chapters in the book, and I recommend you read it **BEFORE** your first meeting.

Create a Probation File

I am one of the most disorganized people you will ever meet. My desk is a total mess. My house is a total mess. I would rather do most anything than find a place for everything.

Do you know who *is* organized? Successful lawyers. They have clearly labeled files, notebooks with color-coated tabs, and fancy briefcases to carry it all into court with them. They are prepared with organized documentation to present their cases.

One area where every probationer needs to be organized is probation documentation. You should create a file (your probation officer certainly has one) with all your initial probation paperwork, every proof of payment, verification of community service work, copies of pay stubs, proof of required treatment or classes, and any other correspondence related to your probation. By doing this, you ensure that so long as you are in compliance you will not go to jail.

Most probation officers are good about filing documentation. The very good ones will file it while you are sitting there or as soon as it comes in the mail. But not everyone is that organized.

Imagine performing public service hours cleaning toilets for eight hours one day. You get your paperwork signed, turn it in to your probation officer, and a couple months later you find out you have a violation report for failure to complete the court-ordered community service. You did it. But he/she lost the paperwork. What would happen when you went to court and said you did the work? The judge would simply ask, "Do you have any documentation showing this work was done?" By having an organized file you could show that the work was done and be on your merry way.

Before I scare you into thinking all probation officers are screw ups who are out to get you, let me say this. This tip is merely a precaution. Remember, probation officers are human, and all of us make mistakes. For the majority of probationers the file would never be necessary. But for that minority, having a file with copies of everything the PO has will be a blessing beyond description.

How to Deal with a Difficult Probation Officer

Most probation officers understand their job is to ensure that the conditions of probation are being met and to report violations to the court. Most are very competent and use common sense. Occasionally, one will mistakenly feel it is their job to interpret the conditions and/or to punish the offender. And a few seem to be a few cards short of a full deck.

Check out this story taken found in an online forum:

> "My first probation officer was a very professional individual who did their duty by the book and to the letter. After a year of weekly visits with my first probation officer, we had absolutely no problems whatsoever.
>
> However in June of 2005, I was transferred to a new probation officer that I was informed would be seeing me on a monthly basis. Since the start of my meetings with my new probation

officer, I have become increasingly concerned about my remaining period due to several factors, starting with:

1. Almost every visit for the first six months I would have to remind my probation officer of what my crime was and that no, it was not involving illegal drugs. I would often have to remind her of my name.

2. She has repeatedly called me in for "problems" as she describes them over the phone. Twice I have shown up to have here asking me questions about people and issues I know nothing about, only to have her realize she has been looking at the wrong file on her computer screen. Her general reaction is "whoops" as I stare at criminal records of other people. Unless I'm completely out of my mind, this is not good behavior of someone in charge of other people's lives.

3. She has called me with urgent home-visit problems several times. In one of the more insane circumstances, she left an urgent message while I was out running errands with a relative of mine. When I returned, I called back immediately and informed her that I was back home. She said she would be over in a few minutes. Upon her arrival she storms into the house, points to the bottle sitting on my cutting board and says, "Mind telling me why there's a wine bottle on your counter?" I incredulously look from her to the bottle and say, "You mean the bottle of balsamic vinegar?" She glares at me, storms over to the bottle, picks it up with a flourish, spins the cap off, and (to my disgust) sticks her nose in the bottle. As she glares at me over the bottle, she mumbles "oh" and puts it back down. As she is walking toward the door, she reaches out for the glass of Pepsi I was drinking and sticks her nose in that. I'm still standing there with my mouth hanging open in disgust and surprise as she pulls out the Breathalyzer. I blow absolutely nothing of course, because I HAVEN'T BEEN DRINKING. The final blow to that fine visit comes when she asks me where I was and whom I was with. I inform her it was my sister, and she asks me what her phone number is. In a fit of absolute confusion, I give it to her. She picks up my phone and dials the number. My sister is back at work. The probation officer proceeds to ask for my sister, and when

prompted to identify herself, she responds, "Ellen, (insert my name) probation officer." I am completely shocked. Now people at my sister's place of business are asking why probation officers are calling her. After the probation officer confirms that I was actually running errands, she leaves with a final comment. "You know, I'm just here to help you. I am flabbergasted beyond words."

Another urgent call came a few weeks ago. My probation officer stops by my home at around 9:00 a.m. I am already off dealing with a busy day. She leaves a message that there is another big problem. I get the message later that day, and she has come to the office at around 7:00 p.m. only to tell me that there was what appeared to her to be a passed-out girl on the floor of my living room and signs of disarray which look like a party went on. She brings me back to my house to meet my guests from overseas who had flown in the night before. My associate's girlfriend stayed sleeping on the airbed in the living room that morning while my friend and I went off to get some work done at my new business location being built. A very awkward situation indeed. So what did she find? NOTHING. Surprise of all surprises, no drugs, no guns, no booze, no terrorists. Her reaction, "You still need to come in and see me on the seventeenth." This is said on March 1.

There have been a range of other odd suspicions, ranging from "Where were you today?" to "Why wasn't your dog barking when I stopped by today?" to "Why didn't I see your footprints in the snow?" I usually answered, "Working," "I don't know, ask the dog," "Because I left the house at 8:00 a.m. as I said," "It started snowing at around 10:00 a.m., and you popped in at 12:00 p.m."

4. Now the real kicker. My last visit in February, my probation officer grudgingly agrees that she will sign the paperwork for the approval of my license being restored as long as today's test comes out clean. Afterward she leads me to the bathroom for my monthly test (which she does give every month incidentally). I enter, and a male probation officer witnesses the sample being taken. As I sit and wait for the usual results, my probation officer informs me that a new test is starting today and that the results will not be ready for another week, and she will be

on vacation next week. I nod with the resignation of someone who is dealing with crazy people. Now the real interesting part comes as I watch her try to figure out which label goes on what and who has to sign where, as well as what top goes on the container and what elements need to be included. She calls another person into the room, and they both lean over this mess to try to figure it out. My probation officer then informs me they haven't had their certification for this test yet, so I'll just have to wait while they figure it out. The other person she brought in to help says that I do not have to wait. My probation officer says I have to sign something. I AM GETTING REALLY WORRIED AT THIS POINT! This isn't like an aptitude test, this is my life, and I'm watching two very confused people fumble with it. Well, they both slap all the stickers with barcodes and numbers all over the bottle and say, "Just put them all on there, more information is better than none." I am totally freaked out by the lack of professionalism or basic competency at this point."

Clearly this is a bias story coming from one point of view, but the scenario is certainly realistic. So the obvious question, what do you do when you get stuck with a difficult PO?

1. **Remain polite**. It is a natural reaction to get defensive when we are threatened. And we should defend ourselves. However, *how* we defend ourselves will determine the outcome. If we start in using harsh and abusive language, you can bet two things will happen. First, the PO will tune you out and not listen to what you are saying and second, they will look for the first opportunity to write a violation report.

   Remember, your PO wields tremendous discretion when it comes to your probation. They can make things very easy or very difficult for you. And let's face it. If you are in defense mode then things are already difficult.

2. **Clearly communicate your concerns and expectations**. Tell your probation officer what is bothering you. "Ms. Smith, I know you have a full case load and deal with jerks all day, but I am doing all that you ask and feel that you are trying to make things more difficult than they have to be. I will continue to comply with my conditions and to show you respect, but I need you to recognize that I am doing what I am supposed to and need to be treated as such."

Or in the above example, "I know you have a big case load, and it is easy to confuse who is doing what, but I have been on probation for over a year with no problems. Also, calling my sister's work and stating to her co-workers you were a probation officer was very unprofessional, and I expect it to never happen again."

3. **Document everything**. If dealing with a difficult probation officer, it is very important that you keep good notes. As soon as you are finished with a meeting, write down the date, time, and everything that was said. If you have a recorder, tape the conversation. In some states you will need the permission of the other party to do this so check your state laws to this regard.

4. **Send a certified letter-return receipt requested.** If your verbal request does not help, then send a certified letter to your probation officer stating the issue and desired resolution. Also, send a copy to their supervisor, judge, and to the state office. Again, be sure to be polite and clearly state what is happening. Don't forget to keep a copy for your records.

5. **Request a new PO**. If there is still no resolution, set an appointment with the supervisor to discuss transferring to a different PO. In small towns this will be more difficult, and there is no guarantee that the new probation officer will be any better.

6. **Make sure no matter what, you remain 100 percent compliant with all conditions and requests of the probation officer while trying to resolve personality issues.** Of course, you should always do this anyways, but if a PO is extending their authority and you challenge them, they could look hard for reasons to write a violation report. If you do what you are supposed to, then that will be difficult for them.

They may make unreasonable requests. Find a way to comply with these requests while you make your appeal to the supervisor. Since you are documenting everything and sending letters if they do issue a warrant, you will be prepared to state your case.

So will doing these things really resolve the issue? Maybe, maybe not. We are dealing with individuals who have there own reasoning behind what they do. One thing we know for sure—if you do nothing, nothing will change.

CHAPTER 2

COMPLY WITH THE
CONDITIONS OF YOUR PROBATION

Mary was a young lady on probation for writing bad checks. At first she was a model probationer. She carried herself well, was on time to her appointments, and made all her restitution payments on time or early. After a while I noticed a change in her appearance and attitude. She still made her appointments but was behind on her payments. Something just didn't seem right. So during a visit I announced I would be giving a drug test. She pitched an absolute fit.

"You can't do that! I'm not on probation for drugs," she stated.

"Rule 8," I replied.

"What's that?" she asked.

"Rule 8, I will not use intoxicants to excess . . . I will not use or have in my possession any narcotic drugs or marijuana . . . I will submit to random drug screens as directed."

As I suspected she failed the drug test.

Learn the Rules

Court is a very stressful and confusing event for most defendants. Lawyers seem to be speaking Latin (they actually are), and all you know is that instead of going to jail, you are on probation.

When you are sentenced to probation you will be given what is usually referred to as a probation order. This order lists all the standard rules you will be required to follow as well as any additional conditions set forth by the judge.

State of Tennessee
BOARD OF PROBATION AND PAROLE
FIELD SERVICES DIVISION
PROBATION ORDER

State of Tennessee   In the_____Court, Division
VS.   _____of_____County, TN
                                       No._____

THIS CAUSE, COMING ON TO BE HEARD before the undersigned Judge, and the above defendant named, having on the_____ day of
_____,20_____ BEEN CONVICTED of the OFFENSE OF _____
and on said date having been sentenced to serve a term of_____ years in the _____
IT APPEARING, however, to the satisfaction of the Court that the defendant is not likely again to engage in a criminal course of conduct and that the ends of justice and the welfare of society do not require that the Defendant shall presently suffer the penalty imposed by law by incarceration.
IT IS THEREFORE, ORDERED and adjudged that imposition of sentence is hereby suspended and the said Defendant is hereby placed on Probation for a period of_____ years, under the supervision of the Tennessee Board of Probation and Parole and its supervisors, such supervision being subject to the provision of the laws of this State

IT IS FURTHER ORDERED that the aforesaid Defendant shall comply with the following general and specific conditions of Probation:
1. I will obey the laws of the United States, or any State in which I may be, as well as any municipal ordinances.
2. I will report all arrests, including traffic violations, immediately, regardless of the outcome, to my Probation Officer.
3. I will not receive, own, possess, ship or transport any firearms, ammunition or illegal weapon.
4. I will work at a lawful occupation and support my dependents, if any, to the best of my ability.
5. I will inform my Probation Officer before changing my residence or employment. I will get the permission of my Probation Officer before leaving my county of residence or the State. I will report immediately within 72 hours, after release from my sentencing hearing, to my Probation Officer.

6. I will allow my Probation Officer to visit my home, employment site, or elsewhere, will carry out all lawful instructions he or she gives, will report to my Probation Officer as instructed, will comply with mandates of the Administrative Case Review Committee, if the use of that process is approved by the Court; will comply with a referral to Resource Center programs, if available, by attending, and will submit to electronic monitoring and community service, if required.
7. I agree to a search, without a warrant, of my person, vehicle, property, or place of residence by any Probation/Parole officer or law enforcement officer, at any time.
8. I will not use intoxicants (beer, whiskey, wine, etc.) of any kind to excess, or use or have in my possession narcotic drugs or marijuana. I will not enter an establishment whose prime purpose is to sell alcoholic beverages (bars, taverns, clubs, etc.). I will submit to random drug screens as directed.
9. I agree to pay all required fees to the Supervision and Criminal Injuries fund unless waived by appropriate authorities. Additionally, if so ordered by the court, I will pay all imposed fines, court costs, and restitution.
10. I will observe any special conditions imposed by the Court as listed below:

11. I will provide a biological specimen for the purpose of DNA analysis, such specimen to be collected and forwarded by the approved agency to TBI, pursuant to TCA 40-35-321.
12. If convicted of a sex offense, I will abide by the Specialized Probation Conditions for Sex Offenders as adopted by the Board of Probation and Parole.
13. If convicted of an offense or an attempt to commit an offense under TCA 39-13-502, 39-13-503, 39-13-504, or 39-13-522, such offense being committed on or after July 1, 1996, I shall be sentenced to and agree to abide by the provisions of Community Supervision for Life, pursuant to TCA 39-13-524.
14. I will not engage in any assaultive, abusive, threatening or intimidating behavior. Nor will I participate in any criminal street gang related activities as defined by TCA 40-35-121. I will not behave in a manner that poses a threat to others or myself
         I have read or have had read to me, the conditions of my Probation. I fully understand them and agree to comply with them.
   I hereby waive all extradition rights and process and agree to return to Tennessee if at any time during my probation the Trial Judge directs me to do so.

_____   _____   _____
PROBATIONER SIGNATURE   WITNESS SIGNATURE   DATE

_____   _____   _____ _____
PROBATIONER ADDRESS   DOB   SS#   SEX   RACE

_____   _____   _____ _____
CITY   STATE   ZIP CODE   TELEPHONE   TOMIS ID
Violation of any of the terms of Probation may be sufficient cause for revocation of Probation.
The expiration date of this probationary sentence is the _____ day of _____ 20 _____
DONE AND ORDERED IN OPEN COURT, this, the_____ day of_____ 20_____

BP0112 (REV 01/2008)   SIGNATURE OF THE TRIAL JUDGE   RDA-1664

Unfortunately, with the stress that comes with the post-sentencing rush to get everything in order, our brains often seem to block out important information. We read the rules of probation or have them explained to us, and then sign documentation stating we understand the rules, but often we retain very little of that information.

That is why it is important to do the following when you are in a less stressful environment:

1. Carefully read both the rules of probation and pay special attention to any additional conditions the judge sets forth.
2. Identify any rules or conditions that will be difficult, or that you will need help with fulfilling.
3. If you have ANY questions about what a particular rule or condition means, make a note and ask your probation officer about it.
4. Start planning how you will meet the different requirements such as:

   a. AA/NA, etc. meetings
   b. Required treatment programs
   c. Public service work
   d. Finding a job
   e. Payment of fines, court costs, and restitution
   f. Providing DNA samples
   g. Registering as a sex offender
   h. Any other condition not mentioned here

Obey the Rules

This seems like common sense but unless you want to go to jail obey the rules. They are there to keep you on the right track and to protect the public. All the rules and conditions must be followed NO MATTER WHAT.

Sure, you *might* get away with going to a bar (rule 8 in TN), but as you well know, bars invite all sorts of trouble. In addition to the obvious risks associated with getting drunk, there's the potential to get into a fight, to take narcotics, or to wake up next to someone ugly. The point is, the rule is there to keep you out of trouble, and if you break it, you could end up serving your full sentence.

You have to make compliance a priority in your life. When preparing a budget, probation fees, fines, and restitution need to be at the top of your list. You need to make time for public service work and required meetings. Avoid environments that can get you into trouble. Make sure you are doing all that is required of you by the courts.

Paying your fines, court costs, and restitution isn't always easy. Money can get tight making it difficult to pay. However, consider this. Do you smoke? If you smoke three packs a week, that is about $50 more a month, you can have if you quit. Plus you get the added health benefits. Do you drink sodas? One a day is easily $1 a day which gives you another $30 a month. Sometimes you may be flat broke, but typically you can pay at least something. I've never known a court to put someone in jail who is making a genuine effort to work toward making their payments. Better to pay something to the probation office than to end up in jail where you can't make any money.

Where will you live? Coming out of prison it may seem the only place to live is with a dysfunctional family. If you live with or near bad influences, then you need to move. The Salvation Army or local mission may not seem attractive, but they can be a great resource for those who need temporary shelter until you can get on your feet. Your probation officer will have a list of resources, so if you find yourself in this situation explain what is going on and that you need help.

Public service work is one area that can be *very* challenging, especially when there are other court obligations such as AA meetings that must be met. Talk to your probation officer about this. My probation officer let me do my work through my church. Many afternoons after work, I would go and pick up trash for an hour. I also helped with Room in the Inn, where I would stay overnight with a group of homeless men. I averaged eight to twelve hours a week during the months that program ran. The important thing again is to put forth the effort so that some hours are put in each month.

Drugs and alcohol use is the most common reason my probationers violated the conditions of probation. I've said it before, but you must not use drugs, period. The judge isn't going to buy the stories about second-hand marijuana smoke or losing your old prescription. If you have a prescription, be sure to make two copies of the label or original prescription. Give one to the probation office and keep the other copy for your personal probation file. Whether ordered by the court or not, if you have a drug problem, get into an outpatient or inpatient treatment program immediately. If you cannot afford one, tell your probation officer what is going on. If you are honest and upfront with your situation, your probation officer is far more likely to work with you to get help than if you fail a drug test and then admit to a problem.

Also, if reporting monthly, don't think that you can smoke a little weed, and it won't show up. For some people it will be out of the system in seven days. For most it takes about thirty days. For me, I gave myself a drug test four days after taking ecstasy to see if it would show up. Not only did I test positive for amphetamines (false positive caused by the ecstasy) but I also tested positive for marijuana. Thing is, I took only a few hits of a pipe, and that was nearly three months before I took the test. That is why it's important NOT to smoke weed at any point after you are arrested.

Alcoholism leads to many violations. I had a man who I truly believed him when he said he had not drunk since the night before. Regardless, he blew a 0.23 on the breath test, nearly three times the legal limit to drive, and I had no choice but to violate his probation. Absolutely do not drink at all the night before a meeting. If you have a problem with alcohol, follow my suggestions on drug addiction and get help.

Report to your probation officer as directed. This is so important; it gets its own chapter. Be sure to read it.

So how is it possible to do all these things? The answer is simple, make a decision! Decide that, no matter what, you will do whatever it takes to comply with the conditions of criminal probation. If that means moving to a different house to get away from drugs or a volatile relationship, then you move. If this means quitting a good paying day job for a lesser paying night job so you can make your criminal probation meetings, then you do it.

Your probation officer cannot violate your probation if you are in compliance with all the conditions of probation. They typically don't want to violate you if you are truly putting forth a GENUINE effort. The point is that no matter what, *you* have to do SOMETHING to work toward meeting your obligations. Trying isn't enough. Listen to the ways of the Jedi as taught by Master Yoda, "Don't try. Do!"

CHAPTER 3

REPORT TO YOUR PROBATION
OFFICER WHEN SCHEDULED

REPORT ON TIME

Tuesday mornings were reporting day at the probation office where I worked. The office was fifty miles from my house, and I had to get up quite early to be at the office by 8:00 a.m.

I set my reporting hours from 8:00 a.m. to 6:00 p.m., and my probationers who were scheduled to report could come any time during the day. I specifically set long hours to allow those who had to work an opportunity to come either before or after work. Yet each week there were those who didn't report.

The typical Tuesday I would arrive about 7:30 a.m., turn on the coffee, and check the voice mail. Each week there would be the same messages from different people.

"Mr. Clay, I have to work and won't be able to come in today."
"Mr. Clay, I don't have a ride."
"I'm sick and won't be in today."

How sad it was that so many people ended up going to jail thinking the above excuses were valid. Sure, if someone was legitimately sick and brought a doctor's note, I would gladly excuse them, after all, I caught the flu from sick probationer's reporting. However, in all too many cases there was no note or a forged note, and certainly the first two excuses were unacceptable.

Why? Because they had notice of when to report.

I cannot stress this enough; plan early, verify your plans, and create a backup plan.

PLAN EARLY

In most cases probation officers give at least a week's notice of when the next report date will be, and often dates are given close to a month in advance. This leaves plenty of time to plan ahead.

Do you work a job that requires you to work during reporting times? If so, arrange to get off early or go in late to your job. Many places will let you stay an extra hour to cover the lost time. You might also be able to take an extended lunch period. If none of those options are plausible, talk to your probation officer well ahead of your scheduled appointment and see if he or she can work with you. Ultimately, it is better to be tardy to work than have your probation revoked.

So many times I would hear the argument, "If I'm late I will lose my job." That might be true, but one thing is for certain, if you violate the terms of your probation and go to jail, you will definitely lose your job. It is better to lose a job and go out the next day to find another than for your family to lose your income for the duration of your jail or prison time.

Another area where you can plan early is transportation. Do you need to take a bus? Make sure you set bus money aside early and forego that extra trip to the vending machine. Also, make sure you take the next EARLIER bus than required. This will allow for the bus being late, traffic, and all the other things that come up. No bus service? Budget a little each week to save for a cab. Do you have a car? Make sure you have gas. Catch a ride with a friend or family member? Contact them early.

If you plan early, then you will be in much better position to get to your appointment. Planning early also lets you know if there are any issues with your plan that needs to be addressed.

VERIFY YOUR PLAN

Two of the most common transportation issues I heard were "my ride can't come get me" or "my ride forgot the appointment was today and has to work."

My response to them and advice to you, "Confirm your plans, recheck, and recheck again!" When you make arrangements for someone to give you a ride, remind them a week in advance. Then remind them the MORNING before, finally remind them the morning of your appointment.

Sure, this may seem like you are nagging, but what are you nagging for? Your freedom! By checking and rechecking you are allowing yourself time to adjust if something comes up and your ride falls through.

This also applies to taking the bus. Unfortunately bus schedules change so make sure you check the schedule a week in advance and also the day before you report.

Verifying your plan is an important tool that will help you to report on time. If something goes wrong, you can adjust your plan or resort to your backup plan.

BACKUP PLAN

In the spring of 1997 I was working as the general manager for a Waffle House. I had built a dependable, efficient weekend crew, and my store was one of the three most profitable stores in the franchise. I was also one of the only managers who consistently hit staffing bonuses for being 100 percent staffed.

I arrived to work early one Saturday morning to plan the day. I rechecked the schedule, and, as always, I had scheduled one extra person than I really needed. About fifteen minutes before the morning shift was to begin, I received a call from one of my waitresses. She would not be in due to illness.

No problem, I thought as I hung up the phone, after all, I planned early and had the extra person scheduled.

Imagine my frustration as she too called out. Saturday morning is a difficult time to call people into work because they are either already snatched up by other stores, or they want the day off. What was I going to do?

I went to my backup plan!

I picked up the phone, called the waitress I had on standby, and covered the shift.

A backup plan is absolutely essential when you are reporting to a probation officer. You need something or someone in place for the rare occasions when all your planning falls through.

If your car won't start or your ride falls though you are prepared. Call mom. Borrow a neighbor's car. Take the bus or a cab. The essential key is to have the backup plan in place.

Notice, in my Waffle House example, my backup plan wasn't to pick up the phone and start looking for a waitress. She was already in place, ready to go at a moments notice. And that is what you need too.

The BEST backup plan for reporting to your probation officer is to set aside funds for a cab. I know in some areas this can be expensive, and bus fare is more affordable, but if at all possible, set aside $5.00 a week until you have at least enough to get you to the probation office. If you keep putting aside money, then you might have money to get home too.

The reason I say this is simple. Typically, a cab can arrive in less than an hour and is MUCH faster than the bus. Thus, if at the last minute your ride does not show up, you can call a cab and hopefully not be *too* late to your appointment.

Also, be sure to call your probation officer and tell them exactly what the problem is, and how YOU are fixing it. If you are legitimately working to solve your issue and explain your course of action "Mr./Ms. Probation officer, my ride canceled on me, but I had cab fare hidden in my shoe in case this ever happened. The cab will be here in thirty minutes and you can expect me by 3:00 p.m."

OTHER TIPS FOR REPORTING

DRESS NICE

When you report to your probation officer you need to dress nice. There is a saying in the business community, "If you dress for success, you'll be successful." We all know that saying is not exactly true, but taking the time to shower, fix your hair, iron your clothes and dress nice gives an appearance that you WANT to be successful. And you need your probation officer to see you as successful—successful in maintaining employment, successful in staying off drugs, successful in rebuilding your life, and successful in complying with your probation.

You don't need to wear a suit and tie each time but something that sets you apart from the other "criminals." This is especially true during your first six meetings. If you report weekly, then this would be for the first six weeks. For those who report monthly this would be for the first six months.

Men, wear khakis and a collared shirt. Women, a dress that comes past the knees or slacks with a nice blouse is appropriate. Also, men should wear a tie for the first few meetings if possible. If you work early in construction or a factory, try to get appointments late enough to allow you to shower before your meetings. If this is not possible, apologize for your appearance and tell your PO you were working.

Obviously, different people have different financial situations. Do the best with what you have. If you cannot afford nicer clothes, wear the nicest clothes you have. Make sure you shower and make yourself presentable. Most importantly, convey an attitude of success.

BRING ALL THE REQUIRED DOCUMENTS

Make sure you bring all required documents when you report. These include the following:

- ✓ Payment for probation fees
- ✓ Proof of payment of fines and court costs
- ✓ Proof of restitution
- ✓ Proof of community service hours worked
- ✓ Proof of required counseling, drug/alcohol meetings, or classes
- ✓ Proof of employment
- ✓ Copy of prescription medication taken
- ✓ Proof of compliance with any other conditions

Sure, the PO could verify some of these on their own, but it is your responsibility to prove compliance. Your probation officer likely has 150-250 people reporting to him or her. There are not enough hours in the week for them to call the courthouse to see if everyone has paid their fines or check the AA rosters, etc. So make sure you bring your proof.

Don't expect them to take your word for it if you don't bring documentation—especially for things like community service or required classes. If for some reason you have complied but the agency could not get you the needed document before you reported, then make a copy of the documentation as soon as you receive it and immediately mail the document, return receipt requested to the probation office. Then follow up with a courtesy call to make sure they received the documentation. Finally, staple the returned receipt to the copy of the document and put it in your personal probation file.

BE RESPECTFUL

This seems like common sense that one would be respectful to the person who holds the keys to freedom in their hands, but some people lacked the self-control or wisdom to maintain control.

I have to admit, as a probation officer, I could be quite insensitive at times. I expected the rules and conditions to be met, and I didn't care for excuses. I could have been a better listener, and now that the shoe is on the other foot, I am actually glad I didn't have myself as a probation officer.

POs are diverse in personality and temperament just like the rest of society. Sometimes personalities mix well, sometimes they clash. Some probation officers might remind you of a counselor or mentor. Some are like a teacher or principle. And some are more like your mother-in-law. Regardless of the personality type, you absolutely MUST maintain a respectful attitude.

You may be thinking, *That's easy for him to say, he's never had Mr./ Mrs.—(you fill in the blank for yourself) as a PO.*

Perhaps, but after being a probation officer and then being on probation for eight years, I have seen pretty much all there is to see. Yes, there are some bad probation officers. I think this is the rare exception, but I know they are out there, and I addressed how to deal with them in an earlier chapter. The important thing to remember is that even if you have the meanest SOB ever, you need to show respect.

Why? Because probation officers are all real, breathing humans with huge caseloads. They have enormous leeway in deciding if someone is complying with the terms of their probation. And, like all humans, they do not respond well when someone shows disrespect.

I can almost guarantee that if you cuss your probation officer or show continuous disrespect, he or she will revoke your probation for the simplest of violations. Forget to mail your payment? Good-bye. Five minutes late to your meeting due to an accident? Pack your toothbrush. Probation officers have to deal with people like us all day long, and where we might punch someone for cussing us, they might simply react by reviewing every detail of your case file to look for any reason to revoke. You must maintain a good attitude no matter what.

Your relationship with your probation officer has great bearing on how your probation will go, and you develop this relationship when you report. All the tips in this chapter are to help you make the impression that you are serious about your probation and that you will follow the rules. Reporting is one of the easiest rules to comply with and one of the easiest to resist. Report on time every time, and you will be on your way to a successful probation.

CHAPTER 4

CHANGE YOUR MIND-SET

Up to this point the focus has been on behavior—keeping a probation file, following the conditions of your probation, reporting on time, being respectful, etc. Our behavior determines our freedom.

If you have ever violated your probation, then you know that doing the right thing is not always easy. So why are some people successful while others are not? What is it that determines our behavior?

The answer is simple. Our way of thinking determines our long-term behavior. Anyone can be compliant short term, but the reality is we must change our mind-set if we are to continue to do the right things.

I have five simple, but not easy, suggestions on how to change your mind-set.

1. Get Rid of the Victim Mentality

When I was arrested my whole world was turned inside out. I was charged with a B felony and was facing eight years without the chance for probation. I would not be eligible for parole for nearly three years. The plea negotiations were agonizing, and the Assistant Attorney General was dead set on us serving three years of actual prison time. I ended up with eight months in jail and seven years of probation.

By the time I started serving my sentence, I was very bitter and angry. I knew in my head that I was responsible for the situation, but my heart was filled with self-pity over how *I* was the victim. In my mind, the police were shady, and the judge was unfair to *me*.

Looking back I can see how my selfishness was to blame. When you are a victim everything is about *you*. It's about how this person treated *you* unfairly, how your job demands too much of *you*, how your probation officer is out to get *you*. But here's a newsflash, life isn't just about *you*. Sure you are a part of this world, but you share it with BILLIONS of other people. When you stop focusing on what is happening *to* you and rather what *you* are going to do for yourself and others life begins to get better. Better because you are focused on what you are doing and not everyone else.

The victim mentality is very self-destructive and if you have that mind-set, if you blame others for your situation, then stop now. You are in control, not them. Make a decision that you, or God, control your destiny, and that you will take responsibility for your life.

2. Apply the Law of Attraction

"Whether you think you can or can't, you're right."

Henry Ford

The law of attraction is really easy to understand but difficult to apply. It simply means what ever you think about will happen.

If I think, *I will not make it through probation,* or *I will never find a good job* or whatever negative thought applies, then that is what typically will come to pass. However, if I say, "I will make it through probation," or "I will find work I enjoy," then that is what will come to be.

Why? Because how we think determines what we do. When I am consumed with thoughts of how broke I am, how I cannot afford food for my kids, how I'm late on rent again, etc. I find it near impossible to find a bit of "good luck." But it has *nothing* to do with luck. It has to do with attitude and motivation.

If I think instead, *I am going to pay all my bills this month,* then I am motivated to make it happen. I will look for a part-time job, cut nonessential spending, and if I am still short, I can ask for help. The point is I am then motivated to *make* something happen, and often good things will just seem to happen out of nowhere.

I took the following example from *www.power-of-giving.com*:

"A child wants a specific gift for Christmas, and he gets it. It wasn't magic. There are a great many things that took place behind the scenes to make this happen: (1) He thought of something that he really wanted. (2) He thought about it a lot. (3) Those thoughts made him take specific actions that ended in his achievement of obtaining his wish. (4) He voiced his wish to his parents, friends, and family. Everyone around him knew what that kid wanted for Christmas. (5) He wrote a letter to Santa, again reinforcing his desire."

Make no mistake, our thoughts are powerful. Depression cripples millions of Americans each year because they can't regulate and balance their thoughts, while others achieve great success setting goals they believe they will meet.

Napoleon Hill is considered to be one of the greatest authors on the subject of success. If you read his writings, they all focus on getting the right mind-set. That's exactly what we need to do. He even suggests writing out your goal and then saying it out loud first thing each morning, and the last thing before you go to sleep. Start with something simple and realistic, then improve on it from there.

For someone just starting out I would say something like, "I will be successful in all that I do, and I will come home a free man for the rest of my life."

Mine has evolved more or less into a mission statement. "I will provide a safe and nurturing home where my children will learn to love themselves, others, and God. And to give them the tools to be successful, honorable women."

You may be asking, "What does that have to do with staying out of jail?" Everything! I can only complete my mission if I am a free man. Because I know my mission, and I am dedicated to fulfilling my mission, everything I do is working toward that goal.

I right this book for three reasons.

1. To help others, and thus teach my kids the importance of making a difference in someone's life,
2. To show that when we make mistakes in life we can always turn things around for the better, and
3. To make money

All three of those reasons relate to my mission statement.

Deciding simply that we will survive probation is not enough. We must think about and focus on our life *after* probation. We must speak our freedom by verbalizing our goal. Then we will surely do all that is needed to see that reality.

3. Stay away from bad influences.

"He that lieth down with dogs shall rise up with fleas."
Ben Franklin

This may be the single biggest challenge you face. Let's face it, to some degree we are all products of our environment. Our home, co-workers, and friends have a huge impact on what we do. So what happens when we get out of jail or court, and go back to the same job, and hang out with the same friends? **We end up in the same trouble!**

The following example is the story of a man I met the week after I finished the draft of this book. It SO exemplifies this point I delayed publishing so it could be included.

> "I drank and partied from the time I was eleven until bout two years ago. I was clean when I was in jail, and I was there a lot. When I was out I did my best to take care of my kids 'cause their momma wasn't in their life, but much of the time they had to stay with the grandparents. {During a stay at Florida State Penn. for stabbing a man, he made the statement} Since then, a lot has happened. I've studied God's word and allowed Him to have rule in my heart. Today, I am working for the chaplain here at Florida State Penitentiary," he wrote. "I'm learning to listen to what God has planned in my life, instead of going my own way."

Any of us who have been in prison or jail all know this type of person, their life is changed, yet two weeks later they are back because they done screwed up again. He was heading that direction when something changed. He hadn't been out of prison long when his eight or nine-year-old son asked him a gentle but powerful question. He continues his story . . .

> "My boy and I were eating breakfast, and he says, 'You don't look too good,' so I say, 'Yeah, I feel sick.' Then he asked me the question, 'Do you think maybe you've been partying too hard?' I had heard that one hundred times before from many

people those exact words but at that moment it hit me I needed to change for good. My daughter agreed to help me get started if I move to her city, and I did. I got involved in a twelve-step program and have now been sober for two years.

"If I hadn't moved, I would have been around the same people that always led to trouble. Cocaine was just a phone call away. And sure, I could walk into any bar in Nashville and score some coke, but that's not who I am anymore. I'm the father of a great kid that I have to make sure does not end up where I was."

I love this story because it shows that intentions and dreams don't just happen the way we envision them. We have to decide we are going to make a change, then do whatever it takes to make that happen, and a big step is removing the old influences.

Unfortunately, even though we are expected to avoid unlawful people, many of us feel like we have no choice. For felons, it is very difficult to get a decent-paying job or to find a reputable place to live. On top of this, if convicted of selling drugs, you may not get government housing or food stamps. It's no wonder why so many people fall back on their friends and family. Not that living with family is necessarily bad, but our old negative influences typically know where family lives or may even *be* members of our family.

I was very blessed in my journey to get back on my feet. My wife at the time was seven months pregnant, and I was determined to start working right away. I was hired as a cook at Waffle House. While the work was good, there were plenty of bad influences around. I worked all night and looked for work all day. Fortunately, my determination to be a good dad kept me out of trouble. Eventually I took a job in a call center as a sales rep. They didn't ask about my criminal background, and I didn't volunteer it. Within two weeks I was the owner's personal assistant, within two months I was the office manager, and a month later the director of operations.

Granted, I had certain advantages. I already had a college degree. My parents didn't live near any negative influences, so I was able to stay with them for two months while we saved for a place. And I had great encouragement from my church family.

I say this not to brag, but rather to confess that this is the one area that was perhaps easier for me than most. Everything I've written to this point and after is based on first-hand experience, except the next paragraph.

If you know your living situation is going to get you in trouble, then GET OUT. Ask your church if they can help relocate you to a different part of town, stay at a mission or halfway house, or ask your probation officer for advice.

Do anything to put up a divide between your old life and the life you want to have. A common phrase in the business world is "You can't do the same things and expect different results."

Whether or not you believe in the Bible, it's hard to dispute the passage in 1 Corinthians 15:33 it says, "Bad company corrupts good morals."

If you hang out with nine guys looking at kiddie porn, you're bound to be the tenth. If three potheads wanted to take my daughters to the movie, I would chase them away with a broomstick before repeating the above quotes,

On the other hand I think the inverse is also true. Good company corrects bad morals.

4. Gravitate toward successful people.

My brother has a saying that I'm sure originated elsewhere, but he says, "If you want to be broke all your life, hang out with broke people. If you want to be a millionaire, hang out with millionaires."

I'll talk about creating career opportunities a little later, but for now let's rephrase that quote. "If you want to go back to jail, hang out with people who break the law, if you want to stay out of jail, hang out with people who obey the law."

I'm talking about *morally* successful people. The person who does the right thing, not to avoid getting into trouble, but because it was the right thing to do. We all know people like that don't we? The kid in class who wouldn't let us copy his homework, the guy at work who's always talking about his religion, the grandma who is . . . well she's grandma what more can I say.

And I'm talking about people with positive attitudes. These people look at each day as being full of potential. They enjoy life and others. They take the lemons in life and make lemonade. We all want to be like them. So why not get to know them? After all, attitudes are contagious.

As a parent I can tell you from experience, I rarely have just one grouchy child. If one is grouchy, both are grouchy. If both are grouchy, then Mommy's grouchy. If Mommy's grouchy, I want to work late!

On the other hand, when I go to pick my girls up from childcare after a bad day, and I see them run up with their big smiles and hugs, it fills my heart with joy. In an instant my attitude is transformed; all because of a smile.

5. Decide to be happy.

Do you ever go to a public place and pause for a bit to do some people watching? You can almost make a game out of guessing what is on someone's mind as they plow down the grocery aisle with the snarl on their face. Or for those of you who Facebook, have you ever noticed how some people are chronically negative? "My back hurts, my feet hurt." "Nobody loves me." "Life is so miserable why do I exist?" Or better yet change their relationship status as soon as a guy smiles at them, and the next day rants at how men were designed to break hearts, sniff, sniff. I want to scream at them, "SHUT UP ALREADY! HAVE YOUR PITY PARTY BY YOURSELF!" or "No crap you're lonely. No one wants to be around your whiney butt!"

I understand that if you are reading this book, you are likely not very happy at the moment, and that is OKAY. I am not happy every day or even every week. I had a two-month period this summer when my stress level was nearing when I was first incarcerated. My stress level was high, but I was still *mostly* happy.

How? Because I decided a long time ago I was going to be happy. And because I believe happiness is not just a feeling of emotion, but rather an attitude of appreciation.

No matter how bad things get for me I remember the good things I have. For me it's my children, my family, and my church and my salvation. Everything else is just stuff and can be replaced. Everything else except my freedom. I value and cherish my freedom. Freedom is what lets me do the things and see the people that make me happy.

If you look on the next page you will see a list I adapted from *Climbing Happiness Hill* by Alan Bryan. Alan was minister at my church growing up, and he penned a number of books. I admired and respected him greatly. He wrote *Climbing Happiness Hill* in the 1970s, and the principles are ringing just as true today.

Keys to Happiness

1. Live the simple life. Be temperate in your habits. Avoid selfishness. Make daily plans simple.
2. Spend less than you earn. Keep out of debt.
3. Think constructively. Train yourself to think clearly and accurately. Store your mind with useful thoughts.
4. Cultivate a yielding disposition. Resist the common tendency to want things your own way. Try to see other's point of view.
5. Be grateful. Be glad for the privileges of life and work.
6. Rule your mood. Create a mental attitude of peace and good will.
7. Give generously. There is no greater joy in life than to render happiness to others by means of intelligent giving.
8. Work with rights motives. The highest purpose of your life should be to grow in spiritual grace and power.
9. Be interested in others. Divert your mind from self-centeredness. To the level that you give, serve, and help will you receive happiness.
10. Live one day at a time. Concentrate on your immediate task. Make the most of today for it's all you have.
11. Have a hobby. Nature study, walking, gardening, music, golfing, stamp collecting, sketching, voice culture, reading books, photography, social service, public speaking, travel, and authorship are samples.

I know that everything in this chapter is easier said than done. In fact, nothing in this chapter is easy which is why so many people violate their probation. Changing how you think, how you view life, and how you see your future may seem impossible, and it probably is impossible to do on your own. So get help, get motivated, and get started on making your new life. If you can do this, then the next few chapters will be easier to do since they all require commitment and change.

CHAPTER 5

SPEND YOUR TIME WISELY

We've all heard this before, "Spend your time wisely," and if you're like me you have probably rolled your eyes on more than one occasion in your life when it was said. But let me ask you something. What did you do today? More specifically, what did you do to better your life, the lives of your family, and the lives of your community? It is so easy to get distracted or even unmotivated in life. There are only two things in life that you can never get back once it's gone; a physical life, and time. Did you know that if you set aside one hour each day that would give you an extra two weeks each year? This chapter focuses on getting the most out of life by making the most of your time.

I once heard the story of a professor who is teaching about time management. He holds up an empty jar and says, "Is this jar full?" The class answers, "No." He then puts some large rocks in the jar and says, "Is it full now?"

"Yes," the class answered.

"Really?" he asked, as he put some small gravel into the jar. "What about now. The class was catching on and watched as he next added sand, and finally water.

When finished with the demonstration he asked, "What was the point of this lesson?" Someone in the class replied, "No matter how little time you think you have, there's always room for more."

"No," the professor said, "the point is if the big rocks don't get put in first, they will never fit."

You may think that organization is the most important part of time management, and it *is* important, but I believe the MOST important aspect is prioritization. We must decide what the most important tasks in our life are and make it a priority to make time for them *first*.

Things like work, school, eating, bathing, and sleeping are some of the more obvious things for which we make time. But other important tasks include making our probation meetings, doctor's appointments, drug and alcohol counseling, children's functions, dating your spouse if married with children, parent-teacher meetings, and the list goes on. We must make time for these things, or our time will slip away.

The other key element in making the most of your time is being organized. For some this comes naturally. Not me. I am, by nature, one of the most disorganized, forgetful people you will ever meet. I forget appointments, birthdays, anniversaries, holidays, and the list goes on and on. The only way I function is by writing the important appointments down (actually I use the calendar function in Outlook) where I can get the constant reminder.

Procrastination

My house is a mess right now. Actually it is almost always a mess. Why? Because the official cleaning day is "tomorrow." So if today is Monday, and the official cleaning day is "tomorrow," will it get cleaned on Tuesday? No! When Tuesday arrives it becomes today and "tomorrow" is the official cleaning day.

Most of us have faced the procrastination demon at some point in our life. It's that little voice that says, "You can do it later." But "later" never comes because something always comes up, or there is always an excuse.

So why do we put things off? In many cases the task just seems too big, and we don't know where to start. Often we delay having to make an important decision because we are afraid we'll make the wrong decision. I would typically put off things that I really don't care for doing, like housework, and instead do something I did enjoy like watching TV or playing poker. The worst procrastination is when you start a project then put off finishing it. Once that happens you've lost that momentum, and it is usually much harder to get that train restarted toward its destination. We still have to do what we have to do, so we might as well do it now.

When it comes to supervised probation procrastination is very dangerous. It is easy if you get paid on a Friday to say to yourself, "I don't want to drive all the way to the courthouse today. I'll pay my fine on Monday." But by the time Monday comes, you are short the full amount and would only pay half. So you say to yourself, "I'll catch it all up next week," but then you are short even more and the pattern continues until you have dug a hole so deep that it will be a very difficult climb.

Another example is turning in required paperwork. It could be that you forgot to bring it with you or that you forgot to pick it up or get it signed in the first place. When you realize you forgot your paperwork you need to stop whatever else you are doing and get it right away before you forget.

Finally we need to make sure we don't push back leaving for our supervised probation meetings. There are so many distractions, so many things we need to do during the day that we often push back when we leave for our probation meetings. Don't! Set a time when you need to leave and stick to it. People are rarely late because they cannot arrive on time. They are typically late because they do not leave on time.

If you are frequently bit by the procrastination bug, do something about it. Decide that completing your supervised probation is the most important thing on your agenda and get it done.

Here are a few tips to help you PLAN your time.

1. Make a list of all the things you need to do in the next month. This will include functions you must attend as well as when you are going to pay your bills (paydays are good to write down too), home project days, outings with the family, etc.
2. Buy an extra large desktop calendar and write down all major appointments first.
3. Try not to plan more than one major function in the same day. If you must, schedule one in the morning and the other in the afternoon or evening.
4. Write down everything else you have planned.
5. Buy a pad of Post-it notes, so you can leave yourself daily reminders where you will see it. (Car mirror is a good place.)
6. Create a daily schedule or routine.

Obviously you are reading this book, which is a good use of time to better yourself!

Acknowledge and Avoid Addictions

I want to start by saying addiction is a bitch! It is a wild dog that seems like your best friend in the beginning but later bites you in the rear and won't let go. You can yell, hit, and try to run, but unless you get outside help, you are typically screwed.

According to the Merriam-Webster's Online Dictionary addiction is "the quality or state of being addicted" and addicted is "to devote or surrender to something habitually or obsessively."

I always thought of addiction as being something limited to drugs or gambling, and even then, having known alcoholics and other drug addicts, I thought that gambling could not really be as addicting as a chemical. However, I now know that a psychological addiction can be even *more* difficult to break than a physical one.

In addition to chemical addiction, I believe the following are also psychologically addictive:

1. Drugs and alcohol
2. Video games
3. Gambling
4. Pornography/Sex
5. Internet
   a. Social Networks
   b. Instant Messengers
6. TV
7. Sports
8. Reading
9. Anything else that you "devote or surrender to habitually or obsessively"

If you have an addiction, make a decision today to stop. Get the help you need from family, church, friends, or counseling, and make the change. Until you are passionate about stopping, the cycle will continue, and you will never succeed in life, much less probation.

Increase Your Knowledge

I don't know about you, but starting about age fourteen I hated school. Actually, I liked the social activities associated with school, but I hated sitting in class. I made mostly good grades but wondered when I would need to know complex formulas or what Walt Whitman was trying to communicate in his poems. But I now see that the real value of high school is that for the most part it teaches you how to learn. And let's face it, life is about learning.

The question is, what do you spend your time learning? When I sold drugs, I learned about weight conversions, chemistry, biology, drug laws, and eventually jail. Others with whom I spent time in jail learned about counterfeiting, how to steal a car, etc. Clearly, the end result was not what we desired, but the fact is we learned *how* to break the law.

Now imagine if you spent the same time, same energy, and same focus on learning something productive. How would your life be different?

When my brother was in jail he read *The Power of Positive Thinking*. He made a decision to spend his nonworking time reading. Since then he has read numerous books, most dealing with marketing and personal success. The results speak for themselves. Ed owns one of the largest mixed martial arts gyms in the country, an apparel company, a drug rehab facility, a real estate investment company, and is a published author. He accomplished this by becoming an expert at what he does and applying the marketing strategies he learned from reading.

You may be thinking that since you have a "regular job" that none of this applies to you. If you think that, you are sadly mistaken. If you are in sales, learn to sell better. If you are a stay-at-home Mom, read books on parenting. If you are in roofing, learn everything you can about roofing. If you hate your job, learn everything you can about something you enjoy and then make a career change!

The only way to change your life is to do something else. The way to do something else is to learn *how* to do something else.

Keep Busy and Avoid Boredom

"If the Devil finds a Man idle, he'll set him at work."
(J. Kelly, "Scottish Proverbs," 1721)

On a late Tuesday night, in late 1999, I was lying in my room listening to music. Everyone else was in bed or gone. I wanted to go to sleep because I had to be at work the next morning, but I was wide awake. Bored out of my mind, one thought kept echoing in my head. *Do some K.* For those who are not familiar with "K," it is short for ketamine, which is an anesthetic used on animals and infants before surgery. The effects are basically a short "trip" followed by relaxation. For me, it seemed the perfect solution to the boredom I was experiencing.

Boredom is a snare we must avoid. When we are idle a number of things take place. First, it allows us time to think. Thinking alone is not a bad thing, but unless we are focused on thinking productively, we will end up thinking on negative things. Things about our self-worth, how messed up our lives are, etc. We also tend to search for ways to fill that boredom. If we are not deliberate in setting our tasks, we risk slipping into old unproductive and potentially negative habits.

On the other hand, if we keep ourselves busy by planning every aspect of our time, we can avoid these pitfalls. If we plan and stick to a schedule such as up at 6:00 a.m., at work by 8:00 a.m., dinner at 5:00 p.m., TV 7:00-9:00 p.m., bed 10:00 p.m., there will be little room for idle time.

We are all busy, and it seems there will never be enough time to do what we want. Life happens, and we get bumped off course. I completed 1/2 of this book in just two months. It is now fourteen months later, and I am just now getting back on course. Had I finished nine months ago, how many more people could I have helped?

But like I said that's life and life happens. My challenge to you is to get the most out of life by making the most of your time.

CHAPTER 6

CREATE CAREER OPPORTUNITIES

One of the most difficult challenges facing someone on probation is what they are going to do for work. Some are able to continue in their present employment. Others find jobs in areas that don't require background checks. But for some, finding work in their area of expertise may prove quite difficult.

When I was released from jail I immediately went to work as a cook for a restaurant chain. I had a college degree and had worked in business management or as a probation officer for years, so the pay was a good but less than what I was used to.

I saw an ad paying $10 an hour in a call center, so I called, set up the interview, and fortunately, they didn't ask about my criminal history. I worked my butt off during my shift and volunteered to assist the owner with his office work when my shift was over. Within a couple of weeks I was his personal assistant. Within two months I was the office manager, and a month later I was the director of operations making a $40K a year salary plus bonuses.

It wasn't easy. I worked sixty to seventy hours a week, I had a six-month-old baby, and I had two hundred hours a year in public service work to complete. But I did it. And you can too.

Good is Good Enough for Now

Are you waiting for that prefect job? Do you have skills that would be undervalued working in fast-food or construction? Do you want to receive great compensation doing what you love? If you answered yes to any of these questions, then you are just like most of the other 9 percent of the population that is currently unemployed.

One of the conditions of your probation is that you work. For someone on probation, especially felony probation, that means you may have to do work that is beneath you in your mind. Fast-food, retail, and pizza delivery are industries that are always hiring.

When I first got arrested, I, of course, lost my job as a probation officer. I had lawyer bills, a $5,000 loan to repay to my parents for my bail, and no income. I went to a local pizza place and delivered pizza for two months. It wasn't easy with my 1976 Datsun with no air-conditioning and a broken driver-side door handle, but I averaged $12-14 per hour. I knew my car wouldn't last, so I started looking for other work while delivering pizzas and eventually started working in a call center.

I easily could have let pride get in the way of work. I was a college graduate who majored in criminal justice and a double minor in political science and psychology. I had years of management experience, and I was working in a pizza place. But work is work, and the work paid. Getting paid was good, and good is good enough for now.

Set Long-Term Goals

We all have to do what we can to get to work right away. Sometimes the work we find is not what we enjoy. That is why I said, "Good is good enough *for now*. We need to plan for better later.

James was a high school drop out. He took a job as a janitor in a factory but had a passion for comedy. He started doing stand-up routines at his school before he dropped out and would do a few stand-up gigs on the side. In 1996, he received the largest up front payday of any comedian in history up to that point, $20,000,000. Had Jim Carrey not had a long-term plan, he would likely still be working in a steel factory.

What are your dreams? What do you enjoy doing? What are you passionate about? Set your one, five, ten-year goals and work toward them. Jim Carrey wrote himself a $10,000,000 check. Why is that a big deal? He wrote it long before he made it in the comedy with the goal of someday being able to cash it.

Whether you stayed with an existing employer or have to start over the following tips will help you succeed.

1. **Be honest**—My employer didn't ask about my past, nor did I volunteer it, but had he asked, I would have told the truth. When I was a cook I was asked about my past, and I explained what had happened. They still offered me a management position at the restaurant. I turned it down due to the required hours, but had I lied I would have disqualified myself had I later chose to enter management.

2. **Work hard**—Lloyd Irvin, a world famous Mixed Martial Arts instructor and entrepreneur says it best, "Hard work always beats talent when talent refuses to work hard." Show your boss that YOU are the hardest worker. That YOU are the most dedicated, and that YOU are the one person that he or she can depend on no matter what.

3. **Learn**—In addition to physically working hard you should also work hard at becoming the best at what you do. If there is a learning opportunity, seize it. Read trade journals, take a night class. Learn all you can about your field. Make it your goal to be more skilled than everyone else.

4. **Be dependable**—Show up to work early and leave late. Don't miss work unless it is a TRUE emergency. I would often show up horribly sick just to be sent home. At least the boss knew I made the effort. Also, hangovers, lack of child care, and family issues are not reasons to miss work. You should have a backup plan for child care well in advance of an emergency. We all have "family issues," so leave them at home and get your tail to work. As for being hung over . . . DON'T, it's a violation of your probation to be intoxicated anyhow, but if you *are* hung over, get to work.

Finally I would like to add that you should be working toward doing something you enjoy. If you enjoy your work, you will be good at it. It is not always possible to do what you enjoy right away. That's why I took the cook's job, but you can work toward that goal.

If you do the four things listed, you WILL be successful. Hard work and knowledge are the two biggest factors an employer looks at when considering a promotion. Honesty is a personal trait that yields its own rewards. And less face it, no one wants someone who is not dependable.

How to Get the Job You REALLY Want

As a convict your job opportunities become more limited. Employers usually ask about your criminal record, and many now do background checks. Although it is illegal to discriminate for a conviction that is not related to the job being applied for, most employers will. So if you tell the truth, you might not get hired, if you lie and later get caught, you will for sure get fired. So what do you do?

For 97 percent of people this strategy won't apply. Most people talk about wanting a better life but stay in the same social groups, same economic class, and same level of job achievement. They complain about how they don't have the same opportunities, the same advantages, and make excuses about why society keeps them down and holds them back. If that is how you feel, you might as well not read the next section. It is for winners—people who will rise in spite of their circumstances. It is for people who choose to make their own destiny and who do not count on others to take care of them. This information is for the 3 percent who will go on to be thousandaires, millionaires, and possibly billionaires.

1. Pick an industry you want to dedicate your life to. Your focus may change over time and should as you develop and evolve, but pick something you enjoy.
2. Learn all you can about the industry, job. Learn what companies in your area are the best at what you want to do. How are they the same, and how are they different.
3. Pick a company to apply to and learn everything you can about that company. I'm talking details. How they got started, the owner or CEO's name, and most importantly, what you have to offer that relates to the needs of the company.
4. Prepare a resume that focuses less on where you worked, but rather what you did and how you benefited the employer. Education and work history is important, but the skills section of the resume is the most important part. Here you can focus on what you are good at regardless of work history. See page 50
5. Create a unique selling position, and focus on it during the interview. Avoid the clichés "I'm a people person," "I'm a team player," etc., and instead give specific examples of what you bring to the table such as "I'm not proud of my drug-dealing days, but the experience gained from selling to a diverse customer base with different personalities will allow me to shine above the rest. Let me prove that my skills are second to none."

6. Ask for the job. I recently hired the best sales person I could ask for. The interview went well, and I was fairly certain he was the right guy for the job, but I wanted to finish the other interviews before making any decision. Before going into the normal "we'll let you know in a few days," I asked him if he had any questions. He gave the best response I've ever heard. He said, "You see what I bring to the table, so the only question I have is, are *you* going to hire me?" I answered "yes" and canceled all the other interviews.

7. Once hired, always be positive. This means *never* talk bad about the company for which you work, and never complain. This doesn't mean that your work is great, it means *you* are great. The Bible in Matthew 12:34 says, "Out of the abundance of the heart the mouth speaks." You have to guard your heart against contempt for your workplace. If you do not, the negative thoughts will consume you, your work will suffer, which will cause more dissatisfaction. If things are *really* that bad, then start looking for a different career but keep positive and your current job.

8. Be the best at what you do. Have your own private competition to outperform your co-workers. No cheating. Be the best because you are the best, and your managers will notice.

9. Develop productive relationships with your supervisors and managers. Many years ago I was training in restaurant management for a well-known chain. I performed above average, but I made sure I was noticed. How? When I realized the district, regional, division, and area managers frequently played golf, I asked my district manager if he wanted to play sometime. We played often, and he beat me often. So then I started playing with the division manager and regional managers. By the time I got my own store I had developed relationships all the way to the owner of the chain. I had been in my store less than two weeks when I was invited to attend the district managers' meetings, and invited to dinner with the owner and area managers. Since they could not officially promote me to district manager that quickly without causing a ruckus, they simply gave me a raise, put another manager in my store, and in less than two months I was more or less a district manager without the title. Had I stayed with the company and not changed careers I would have advanced faster than anyone in the history of the company. Was it because I was that good as a store manager? Yes, I was good, but it was the positive relationships I created with the decision makers that made the difference. You might be saying, "I ain't

kissing nobody's butt." Fine, don't. Be like the 97 percent of the population that are content to stay where they are. But if you want to be successful, you *have* to develop these relationships. And I'll tell you a secret. When you have a positive (butt kissing) relationship with the decision makers, they listen to you and *act* when you have a problem.

10. Always be Learning (ABL) No matter what you do in life, no matter how good you are, no matter what you already know, you need to always be learning. This means different things for different people. I have had several career changes, and always build on my knowledge. For the past couple years, I've been learning so much this book has seen numerous delays. In the past year alone I've learned how to design websites, write advertising sales letters, been to two industry training conferences, I can get a website ranked on the first two pages of Google within one day, learned to edit and produce videos, and am now learning special effects so I can create short movie clips for my brother's martial arts school. In one year I have made myself an expert in advertising so that if my regular job disappears tomorrow, I can quickly find other work. Do I sound cocky? Well, I'm not. I'm confident. The difference is a cocky person thinks they are better than someone else when they are not. They are a prime target that everyone wants to bring down. I'm confident because I know I am good at what I do because of what I learned. If you are in roofing, learn all you can about residential roofing first, then move to commercial. Are you a mechanic? Learn all you can about a specific skill such as breaks and become the expert in your area on brakes. No matter what you do, **A**lways **B**e **L**earning!

```
Examples for a resume

Criminal Enterprise
"Effective manager of _____ employees"
"Superior accounting and business management"
"Goal oriented team leader"

Selling Drugs
"Created order fulfillment system"
"Organized distribution network"
"Established supreme customer service and sales
process"
"Provided customers with information on product
features."
"Closed sales."
"Provided resolutions to customer issues."
"Researched and revised product content."
"Maintained vendor relations."
"Continuously raised close ratio through effective
training and motivation."

Theft
"Creative problem solver"
"Keen sense of observation, attention to detail"
```

When it comes to being successful in your work, there is too much involved to put it into one chapter. There are volumes of books available on the subject. I recommend that everyone read *Think and Grow Rich* by Napoleon Hill, and *How to win Friends and Influence People* by Dale Carnegie. The goal of this chapter is to get you started on a successful career. Follow these tips, and you will be on your way to a better life.

CHAPTER 7

GIVE TO YOUR COMMUNITY

Why should you volunteer?

It feels great. The gratification that comes from serving others is an important reason to volunteer. Whenever you commit your time and effort to an organization or a cause you're passionate about, the reward of fulfillment can be eternal.

Helping others strengthens your community. Locations that use volunteers are providing important services at low or no charge to those that require them. When a society is performing well as an entirety, its people are better off too.

Volunteering is a great way for families to enjoy time together and feel closer. Some people say they don't have the time to volunteer with so many functions and family commitments. If that's the case, try rethinking how to spend some of your free time. You can select just one or two projects a year and make them a family tradition (for instance, generating and donating gift baskets to care facilities for the elderly around the holidays).

What You Can Discover from Volunteering

If volunteering begins at an early age, it can turn out to be component of your lives—something you may just anticipate and wish to do.

Give to your community today and learn:

1. A sense of responsibility. By volunteering, people learn what it means to create and maintain a commitment. They learn how to be on time for a job, do their best, and be proud of the outcomes. But they also discover that, ultimately, we're all responsible for the well-being of our communities.
2. That one person can make a difference. A fantastic, empowering message for probationers is that they're important enough to have an impact on somebody or something else.
3. The benefit of sacrifice. By giving up an item to a less-fortunate person, we learn that occasionally it's good to sacrifice. Cutting back on recreation time to help clean up a beach tells us that there are essential things besides ourselves and our immediate requirements.
4. Tolerance. Working in community service can bring us in touch with people of different backgrounds, abilities, ethnicities, ages, education, and income levels. We learn that even the most diverse people could be united by common values.
5. Job abilities. Community service can assist young individuals decide on their future careers. Are they interested in the medical field? Hospitals and clinics often have volunteer programs. Do they adore politics? Probationers can volunteer on the actual campaigns of local political candidates. Studying to work as a team member, taking on leadership roles, setting project goals—these are all abilities that may be gained by volunteering and will serve probationers well in any future career.
6. How to fill idle time wisely. If children aren't involved in conventional after-school activities, community service could be a wonderful option to do something as a family.

Volunteering on your own

If you have by no means been involved in community service prior to being ordered to by the court, ask your probation officer for ideas. Wish to improve your PC (personal computer) understanding? You may get free on-the-job training. Have you been out of the workforce due to incarceration or drug abuse? Volunteering may be a painless way for you to get back into the routine of working before taking the plunge into a paid position.

And if you are searching for a career change, community service is really a networker's dream. You are able to meet people who might offer opportunities you've by no means thought of. You are able to sample different workplaces and see how you like numerous fields. Your volunteering will certainly help others and may help you too.

Get Your Family Members Involved

The web offers plenty of sites with info about volunteer opportunities. You are able to also call a favorite charity, hospital, or church directly to see if they've any needs, or look up "Volunteerism" in the phone book in the Human Services section (frequently within the blue pages).

Or get in touch with a local volunteer clearinghouse, which matches up volunteers and community organizations and can help you discover openings at nonprofit organizations in your area.

Be ready to answer questions such as:

- What are your interests?
- What are your abilities?
- Do you have any unique requirements?
- Do you have a method of transportation?
- How many hours a week do you have to volunteer?
- Why do you would like to volunteer?

You will most likely be interviewed again as soon as the clearinghouse matches you with a suitable job. Some situations need more information. In the event you want to function with children, for instance, you may need to undergo fingerprinting and a criminal background check.

Be sure to be just as thorough whenever you question the organizations. Discover exactly what's expected of you prior to your accepting the volunteer position. Be realistic and ask particular questions.

When searching for a volunteer position, keep in mind that it may be challenging to discover the perfect volunteer slot. Be flexible and keep searching if the agency you were referred to doesn't meet your needs. It might take a while to find a perfect fit, but once you do, it'll be worth it.

Once you do become involved, be responsible to those that depend on you. Be on time, dress appropriately, and let the volunteer coordinator know in the event you can't make it. Whatever you choose to do, volunteering and community service can benefit both the community and your family members. Get involved today!

FINAL THOUGHTS

The journey through probation is not an easy road. There are many bumps, potholes, and curves along the way. Nearly half the people who start the trip never make it to the end. They break down, run out of gas, or just flat out chose another route. That is why it is so important to use all the tools available and make sure you are prepared. On a long road trip, you have to pack, make sure you have your oil changed, and good tires. You have to plan the most efficient route, then you have to obey the traffic laws once you get going.

The same is true on probation. You have to set a good first impression, attend your regular probation meetings, comply with the conditions of your probation, and put a plan for success in place.

Hopefully, this book will help set things in motion. If you apply the principles learned, you will almost certainly succeed both on probation and in life. I am not some criminal scientist coming up with a complex theory that is unproven. I've been there. I've experienced the emotion, the embarrassment, and the fear. I've experienced the injustice of the justice system. I'm on my way back to court because I learned that although I was sentenced to eight years, the clerk entered the judgment into the computer wrong, adding nearly a year to my sentence, and my probation officer is bound by the state's computer.

Am I angry? Absolutely! Did I cuss my probation officer or go out and violate the terms of probation since my time was supposed to be expired?

Heck no. Why? Because it wouldn't be right. And when it comes down to it, that is what life is *really* about. Choosing to do what's right because it's right, not because someone is looking. Choosing to do what's right because that is what I want my children to learn. Choosing to do what's right because I am a different person, and losing is *not* an option.

If you take one thing away from this book, let it be the desire to win. All the tips, advice, counseling, and knowledge are useless if you don't care. This book is only useful if you care. So go out, implement, and succeed.